I0567961

Maybe
Next
Time

Gabriel Alejandro

THE
OCEAN DEEP

Maybe Next Time by Gabriel Alejandro

Copyright © 2022 Gabriel Alejandro

For permissions contact: gjandro04@gmail.com

Illustrations by Dillon Conroy

ISBN: 978-1-957674-00-1 (print)
978-1-957674-06-3 (electronic)

Published by The Ocean Deep Publishing

13833 Dumfries Rd, Manassas, VA 20112

Printed in USA

For the party people of room 1313

Contents

You Deserve More

Because you fought viciously for the right to just be happy.
And what to show for it?
Ashes and pill bottles and balled up tissues,
a personal civil war museum.

When the moon rose to fill your sky,
no one held you to protect you from the cold.
You learn to cling so steadfastly to the darkness,
and your eyes adjust so much to the shadows
that you cannot tell when it will be day again.

Your skin hardens,
forgetting the brush of fingers against your chest,
or lips on your cheek.
Muscles atrophy,
without another hand in yours.
I know that you feel so weak.

You are a masterpiece, handcrafted.
I know when you look down,
you see yourself cracked and broken,
fractures that glow bright red in your eyes.
But in mine, they run like streams flowing gold and silver
across your stomach, your waist, your arms.
Light dances on your hips, licking up your back,
wrapping in ribbons down your legs.

You are a beacon, a solar flare,
bouncing off the surface of so many worlds.
Leaving a comet trail that twinkles in the eyes of many.

Daybreak is coming, I promise,
and your scars will never tell the whole truth,
so turn around and face the sun,
because you have never been so beautiful.

rainbow baby

my older brother's heart was too big for his body

a mother's love entrenched
in the need to create something new
to grow
to root
into something real

one year later, a daughter.

a mother's heart so devout.

spectate

at the end of the pool where my feet
could no longer touch the bottom
my brother forces my head under the water
testing how long i could hold my breath

eyes shut tight against the stinging chlorine
my heartbeat pumps in my ears
slowing as my lungs plead for release
my frenzied thrashing was no match
for the strength of his hands on my shoulders

when he finally lets go
i breach the surface for a reviving breath
scan for someone who would tell them to stop
but my cries are lost in poolside clamor

later i always thought that my mother
remained a passive bystander
but when i tell her the story
she says she doesn't remember
because she wasn't even watching

first sting

at recess in 2nd grade
playing under a tree next to the playground

dandelions trembled in the breeze
wood chips scattered under light up sneakers

i felt an unfamiliar sting
as my knee landed to crush an unlucky bee

abandoning its lifeless body in the grass
i remember it didn't hurt as much as i thought it would

gatorade

i was in ninth grade
the first time i snuck out
ten pm
november

headlights slice through me
my shadow seeps into the sidewalk

bundled
two hoodies
two pairs of socks
i walk to food lion
just before closing

it stands
a monolith
rinsing the pavement
with buzzing
corporate-controlled lighting

i fill my arms
with all the gatorade i could afford
my triplet babes
lemon-lime
strawberry-watermelon
and my favorite
glacier cherry

late night breeze
grasps at my cheeks
as i raise strawberry-watermelon to my lips
and the other two wait in a plastic bag
that hangs by my knees
while i tip my head back for a sip

the bag stretches
breaks
dumping the two bottles onto the sidewalk
and i wither with a sob
when i see the only one that spilled
was glacier cherry

my childhood home
(according to google maps)

they repainted it. added a fresh front porch. a garage.

i'm sure they painted over the marker from when i learned to spell
my name.
and ripped up the pink carpet i picked when i was three.

i have to wonder,

how many childhood homes i have stripped apart.

and who is looking at my front porch on google maps—

Benji

I promised I would never leave you
Holding you through your final breath
Wrapping you in a scrap of an old t-shirt
Your eyes wouldn't close
I had to put you in the freezer
Because it was 2:30 am

Roots snag on the rusty shovel
I scrape a hole into my backyard
The dirt dry with February air
You looked so peaceful but
Your eyes wouldn't close

Drown

Suspended,
Breathless,
I wonder,
What is out there
What is left

My throat swells,
A vacuum,
My veins tie into knots.

What happens when my heart gives way?
When bloodless lungs fall from empty bodies?

Does the sea offer her loving embrace?
Opening arms of black and blue,
Will she cradle me, gently rocking,
Until my chest no longer yearns to be full?
Am I swallowed,
Dissolved into a murky expanse

Or does the sky reach down with cold hands?
Does the universe wrap fingers through bones?
Twisting through my ribcage,
Am I untangled,
My body weaved back into the stars?

Am I enveloped by the ocean?
Am I sprinkled through the universe?

Space

There is no space for you here.

People like us. We break our hands reaching for things we have no business even looking at. And while we shed tears to stain our streets , they sweep their sidewalks of the dirt from my shoes.

They are haters of love. Catalysts of sameness. Builders of walls upon gravesites. A neighborhood that quickly becomes a necropolis.

They do not unlatch their doors for those hands are too weak to knock. Who stitch themselves together but never stop being torn apart.

We are ragdolls, sock puppets, DIY Etsy projects made from scraps in your kitchen drawer. Should we disintegrate in the back of the cabinets or risk everything to not be forgotten?

There is no space for me? So I will make some. I am my best friend. Unapologetically selfish. Insufferable and bitter. Your comfort with my identity is not my business. I do not fluff pillows for the chronically asleep. I do not bus tables for the willingly starved.

It may be in corners and closets, but there has always been space.

—There will always be space.

The First Time My Father Was Proud of Me

When I first met my manager I hated him.
When I first met my manager, he reminded me of my father.

I finished 8th grade with a 3.98 GPA.
Reading my report card proudly on the living room couch, my
father's only response
Should have been a 4.0

I told him my dream school was the one my mom got her master's at,
he told me
only drunks and partiers go there.
And when I find myself alone with him,
a silent clock ticks, counting down until he tells me I should do
better.
 — he never finished high school.

Today was my last day of work.
I clocked out at 10:19, my manager stuck out his hand to me.
*If you ever need a recommendation put my name down. Good work
tonight*
You're a good kid.'

Immortal

You are a blinking star, falling towards a glowing horizon,
composed of recycled molecules and gasses.
The same ones that make the air we breathe,
the ground we walk.
Your soul has seen an eternity,
felt a million emotions.
Death has kissed your cheek countless times.
You don't remember.

But I am an ancient mammal,
traversing shadowed forests under towering trees.
I am a primordial crustacean,
roaming the ocean floor, practically immortal.
I am a household dog.
I am a boy born into a wealthy family.
I am an aging farmer sweating beneath the sun.
Death has whispered in my ear countless times.
I remember.

You've lived a million lives,
and I will search for you for a million more.

Obglitory Poem About Daddy Issues

I take comfort in knowing that you will never read this book.
Mom will buy it, and by the time she reaches this page she will be crying.
You *might* ask her what's wrong, but she won't answer.
And when she's done, this book will grow dusty on the shelf in the corner of the office.
I take comfort in knowing that I might profit from this poem, that I can create
something meaningful from a relationship so meaningless.

Don't think I didn't notice, you stopped saying you loved me
after I changed my name, stopped coming to my concerts when my voice started to drop,
stopped looking in my eyes when I grew a beard.
We're not technically estranged, but already strangers.
Yet you remain an almost ghostly presence, haunting every corner,
tainting the atmosphere, leaving a spoiled taste to the air.
We should be bound by blood, but you're more like a roommate who pays my phone bill.

It's weird being seventeen and liking school more than home, a freak
who dreads the snow day and rejoices at the Monday morning.
I get good grades, not because I even care anymore, but because it's all you've ever said I'm good at.
My commute home becomes a final desperate breath, bracing myself to hide in bed, in oversized hoodies, drowning myself under dim lights until I can finally feel safe enough to fall asleep

Lottery tickets scattered about the house, watching from the backseat of the car while you pick through trash at a 7-eleven, muffled shouting when my brother walked in late with bloodshot eyes.
Something about those memories, they inhabit all my quiet moments.
But there are no quiet moments in this house.

I take comfort in knowing your hands will never dirty this page, but a part of me almost wishes you would.

This part that wishes I could have been the son you took on fishing trips, that you taught to ride a bike, how to shave.

The same part that knows that I don't want you at my wedding, but wishes I someday would.

For my sake, I hope I will discover some forgiveness tucked away somewhere. To learn that love is not transactional, that hearing a key in the door should spark joy, not panic.

For my sake, I hope that I am at least better for this, that your reflection will never look back at me in the mirror. That I will never poison my household the way you did yours.

This is Not a Love Poem

In 9th grade my writing teacher told the class that dating in high school is stupid.
I have not attempted to write a love poem since.

I *could* write 14 lines about the things I love about you
But this is not a love poem
I *could* tell you that I knew I loved you after our second date
That I practiced telling you after you fell asleep on the phone
That you make me want to do things I would never do
Like go out on weekends
And sit through movies I don't understand

I'd give you my inhaler
give you the air straight from my lungs.
I would stand in the rain to wait for you
I fucking hate the rain.

I could tell you that you made me realize
That I am a whole, real person
With such big feelings, such big thoughts
That it's possible to find people who want to hear them

But this cannot be a love poem
Because presenting myself to you in this way
I am naked, peeling back layers of skin
In your arms, I am at your mercy completely
Do what you will, I'll bleed for you

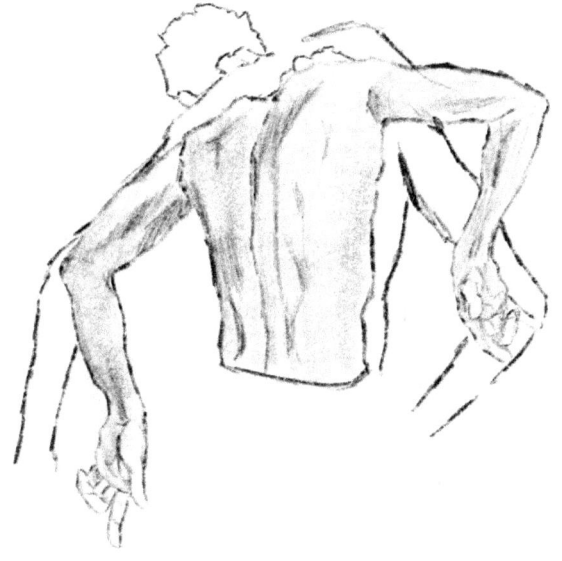

Search History

Everyone says not to *run* from your past
But I swear I am just taking a leisurely stroll
I think I live comfortably, on the edge of seventeen
Beautifully strong, terrifyingly weak.

My therapist asks me to describe things with *feeling words*
I click through thesaurus.com in my head
It's bookmarked, between daydreams about boys and what's for dinner
But I cannot remember enough to know what to put in the search bar

When he asks me to remember, I find my vision grows fuzzy
Light leaks from my memories
Childhood swallowed by a spiraling list of diagnoses
I find myself grasping desperately
But the times before now slip from my fingers

I can do nothing but look ahead
So maybe I am running from my past
But I forgot my inhaler
And I'm not stopping to breathe

4/11

If you had asked me five years ago if I would make it to my high school graduation, I would have said no. The thought of myself past age fifteen had become TV static. Buzzing, crackling, then fizzling out. The path to adulthood is desolate and broken. Road blocked by barriers I have been building since birth.

I grew up petrified by the fear of loneliness. At night I clutter my room with as much noise as possible. Dirtying the air with sound pollution, I must bring my thoughts to extinction. My laptop sits at the edge of my bed, sheltering me from the abuse of my unrelenting inner dialogue. Being alone is so loud…

My high school graduation is in 2 months. I got accepted into my top choice university. I have a boyfriend and so many friends. The path to adulthood is messy, full of debris. My feet are ever-clumsy, but carry me on. Night time still scares me. Some days my head still buzzes. Breathing has not gotten any easier. But the future does not seem so desolate now.

TITLE HERE

I've been telling all my friends
Buy my book, it comes out in May
I'll give you a signed copy
Maybe even a discount

But I forgot to tell them
The content isn't pretty
This has nothing to do with you
But you can at least pay full price
For my quiet suffering

Tunnel Vision

Eye contact has always been hard for me.
I search frantically for somewhere to look
When eyes lock, it sends shockwaves down my spine
Heart palpitations clog my throat
My breath only comes back to me when I can look away.

When I met you I knew that you had blue eyes just like my father.
That looking at you would splinter right through my body and leave
me crumpled at your feet.

But you hold my face in your hands, trail your fingers along my weak
hint of a beard.
My ears get hot when I reach for you and bump your glasses instead
I realize that we've been making eye contact for what feels like hours.
And it doesn't even hurt.

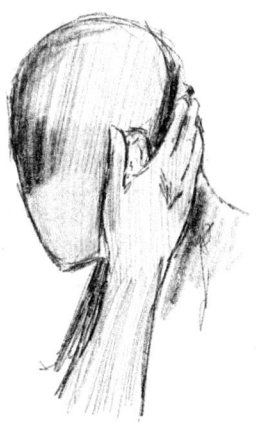

Maybe Next Time

In my kindergarten yearbook picture
I did not smile.
I can imagine my mother searching so many stores for the collared
turtleneck I was wearing.
Because when she put me in normal turtlenecks I could feel my
throat closing in,
I always insisted that I couldn't breathe.

In my kindergarten yearbook picture,
I did not smile,
but I know I thought I was beaming.
I still practice in the mirror before every picture day,
before I met my date for the 8th-grade dance,
while I did my hair for my senior portrait.

I recite my routine mantras about how handsome I am.
Trying to commit to muscle memory what my smile is supposed to
feel like.
Like remembering how it feels to ride a bike.
Because when I try to stretch out a genuine grin,
sometimes my face stays blank.

I sit looking at my kindergarten yearbook photo,
A mirror that I can never spray clean.
My morning pep talks fall out of my mouth, because I have no idea
who I am looking at.
I can only ask, hope, beg
to somehow reach that unsmiling face.
But there are so few words that can heal the pain created by ones left
unsaid.

To me, who tried so hard to smile but never could,
I plead
take back your youth.

From the relentless grip of a tormented childhood.
Chapped cheeks from wiping tears,
hiccuped sobs;
Mom. I. Can't. Breathe.

I am sorry.

But I need you now more than ever,
and I never loved you like I should have.
Because while we continue to drown,
birds still sing,
cattle graze quietly on grass,
and bees still bumble lazily under trees at school playgrounds.

And I hope
when my time in this body is up,
that I might get another chance.
Maybe next time I can come back.
As a bird serenading the rising sun,
a cow getting filled on a summer pasture,
or a bee stinging children at recess.

Maybe next time things will be different.
Maybe next time I will love you like I should have.

Acknowledgements

"Drown" and "Immortal" first published in The Megalodon.
"You Deserve More" and "Gatorade" first published in Siren.

There are many people I would like to thank for helping me reach a point where I could finish this book.

My Class of 2022 classmates in the Creative Writing program at Colgan High School. Having a community of writers to grow and learn with is an opportunity that I will forever be grateful for. I am eager to see what you all will do with your immense talent and potential. The friendships I have made through our shared passion for writing are unforgettable. I will be first in line at your book signings.

My friend Dillon Conroy, who collaborated with me on the illustrations in this book, because what I have in poetic talent, I am greatly lacking in artistic capability. For inquiries Dillon can be contacted at dillon.conroy@yahoo.com.

My amazing creative writing teacher, Ms. Jessica Dyche, who helped cultivate my skills and watched me blossom into a confident writer. After being discouraged by people who didn't understand me, being in your class for the past three years gave me confidence in my craft that I never had before. I am so fortunate to have met you. I hope you felt as much joy watching me grow as I did learning from you. I just know that as long as you are teaching you will inspire so many students like me. I can't wait to see what you do with your own work. I wish you luck in all your future endeavors. I give you a million thank you's for everything.

Lastly, I am, of course, thanking myself. My younger self, for experiencing so many things you would not understand until later and still pushing through. My teenage self, for doing so many things yourself that you should not have had to face alone. And my future self, who I finally have high hopes for, and I know will do great things. Thank you to me; I could not have done this without you.

Gabriel Alejandro is a graduate of the Creative Writing Program at Colgan High School's Center for the Fine and Performing Arts in Manassas, Virginia. He is a former production editor of *The Megolodon* and *Siren* where his work has also been featured. He is an undergraduate student at Michigan State University focusing on environmental studies.